SPACE MISSIONS

BY ARNOLD RINGSTAD

Published by The Child's World®
1980 Lookout Drive • Mankato, MN 56003-1705
800-599-READ • www.childsworld.com

Photographs ©: NASA, cover, 1, 3, 6, 7; JPL/Cornell
University/Maas Digital/NASA, 2, 16; Olga
Zinovskaya/Shutterstock Images, 4; JSC/NASA,
8, 14; Dmytro Bochkov/Shutterstock Images, 9
(rockets); JPL/NASA, 9 (Earth); Shutterstock Images,
10, 21; JPL/Space Science Institute/NASA, 12; KSC/
NASA, 13; JPL-Caltech/MSSS/NASA, 17; Langley/
JPL/NASA, 18; Robert Markowitz/NASA, 22

ISBN 9781503844766 (Reinforced Library Binding)
ISBN 9781503846159 (Portable Document Format)
ISBN 9781503847347 (Online Multi-user eBook)
LCCN 2019957738

Printed in the United States of America

About the Author
Arnold Ringstad loves reading
about space science and
exploration. He lives in Minnesota
with his wife and their cat.

CONTENTS

Yuri Gagarin, a Russian astronaut, was the first human to go to space. He flew in the Vostok spacecraft.

CHAPTER ONE

MISSIONS WITH PEOPLE

Missions into space are exciting adventures. Some space missions have people on them. Others use machines called space **probes**. A few of these probes can even land on planets. They can drive around. These probes are called **rovers**.

The first mission with a person launched in 1961. It was called Vostok 1. Yuri Gagarin was inside the **spacecraft**. He flew around Earth once. Then he returned home safely.

Apollo 11 is the mission that first ▶
took U.S. astronauts to the moon's
surface. The three astronauts
flew on a Saturn V rocket.

Many more
missions followed.
One of the most
important missions
launched in 1969. It
was called Apollo 11. This
mission launched on a huge
rocket called a Saturn V. Three **astronauts** flew
to the moon. Two of them landed on the moon's
surface. They were Neil Armstrong and Buzz
Aldrin. The third astronaut waited in the moon's
orbit. His name was Michael Collins. Armstrong
and Aldrin walked around on the moon. They
picked up rocks and dust. The astronauts
brought these things back to Earth so scientists
could study them.

In the 1980s, people used a new kind of spacecraft. It was called a space shuttle. It launched on a rocket. It flew into space. Then it came back to Earth and landed like an airplane. Space shuttles flew many missions. One of the biggest was in 1990. The shuttle *Discovery* brought the Hubble Space Telescope into Earth's orbit. This telescope looks deep into space. It continues to help scientists learn many new things.

Buzz Aldrin (pictured) and Neil Armstrong were the first people to walk on the moon.

▼

Today, astronauts work on the International Space Station (ISS). This is a huge laboratory in space. There are places to work, sleep, and eat. One important mission on the ISS started in 2015. Astronaut Scott Kelly flew to the station. He lived there for almost a whole year. In 2016, he came back to Earth. Scientists studied him. They learned more about how space affects the human body.

DID YOU KNOW?

The ISS is made of many parts. These pieces were launched separately. Astronauts joined them together in space. The ISS has more room inside than a six-bedroom house!

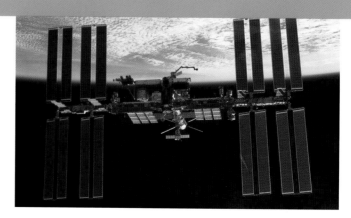

GETTING TO SPACE

ORBIT

FLIGHT PATH

▲ Getting to space is about more than just going up. Rockets start
off pointed upward. But they soon begin turning sideways.
Most of a rocket's energy is used to increase its sideways
speed. It needs a lot of this speed to go into orbit.

The Soviet Union launched
Sputnik 1 on October 4, 1957.

CHAPTER TWO

MISSIONS WITH SPACE PROBES

The first space probe was *Sputnik 1*. It launched in 1957 and went into orbit around Earth. *Sputnik 1* was a metal ball about 2 feet (61 cm) across. It collected information about space for scientists. It also proved that it was possible to launch a probe into space.

Scientists worked on new space probes. Newer probes could fly deeper into space and collect more information. Two of these improved probes were *Pioneer 10* and *Pioneer 11*. *Pioneer 10* launched in 1972. It reached Jupiter after more than a year. *Pioneer 11* launched in 1973. It also visited Jupiter. But it went on to study Saturn, too. The *Pioneer* probes took the first close-up pictures of these two planets.

Cassini took this picture ▶
of Saturn in 2009.

More probes into deep space followed. One was *Cassini*. It flew to Saturn. The probe launched from Earth in 1997. It finally reached the ringed planet in 2004. *Cassini* took amazing pictures. It studied Saturn's moons. It helped scientists learn even more about the planet.

DID YOU KNOW?

Cassini carried a smaller probe called *Huygens*. This probe landed on Titan, one of Saturn's moons. It sent back pictures and information for about two hours, until its batteries ran out.

Cassini was launched on October 15, 1997 on a Titan IV/Centaur rocket. ▶

CHAPTER THREE

MISSIONS WITH ROVERS

The first-ever rover ever was called *Lunokhod 1*. It landed on the moon in 1970. Scientists controlled it from Earth. *Lunokhod 1* took pictures. It studied the moon's soil. It drove more than 6 miles (10 km) on the moon.

DID YOU KNOW?

Some of the astronauts who walked on the moon brought rovers along, too. The astronauts drove the rovers around like cars. This let them explore more than they could by walking.

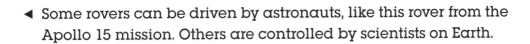

◄ Some rovers can be driven by astronauts, like this rover from the Apollo 15 mission. Others are controlled by scientists on Earth.

Many rovers have also explored Mars. The first was *Sojourner*. It landed on Mars in 1997. It was a small rover, about the size of a remote-control car. *Sojourner* explored Mars for 83 days. It took photos and studied the surface.

The next Mars rovers were *Spirit* and *Opportunity*. These twin rovers landed in 2004. They were bigger and better than *Sojourner*. The rovers were planned to last for 90 days. But they both kept working for several years. *Opportunity* lasted the longest. It sent its final message to Earth in 2018.

◄ This artist's vision of *Opportunity* shows it on Mars. *Opportunity* sent its last transmission to Earth on June 10, 2018. It lost contact due to a storm.

Curiosity was programmed to sing "Happy Birthday" to itself on its first anniversary of arriving on Mars.

Curiosity was the next rover to land on Mars. It arrived in 2012. *Curiosity* is the size of a small car. It carries many scientific tools. It can drill into rocks. It studies the weather on Mars. It even blasts rocks with a laser to study what's inside. *Curiosity* was still driving around on Mars in 2019.

CHAPTER FOUR

FUTURE MISSIONS

Scientists are planning many exciting missions for the future. Some of the missions will involve traveling to the interesting moons of Jupiter and Saturn. Europa Clipper is one of these missions. It will send a probe to Europa, one of Jupiter's moons. Europa has an icy shell. It may have an ocean underneath. Europa Clipper will teach scientists more about this strange moon.

Another future spacecraft will go to Titan, one of Saturn's moons. The spacecraft is called *Dragonfly*. It looks a bit like the **drones** people fly for fun on Earth. This spacecraft will land on Titan. Then it will fly from place to place. This will let it study many areas on Titan.

◀ Scientists are working on Europa Clipper. This antenna model for the spacecraft was tested in April 2019.

Scientists are excited to learn more about Titan. This moon has sand dunes, like those in deserts on Earth. It also has rivers and seas. However, these are not filled with water. Instead, they are rivers and seas of a chemical called methane. *Dragonfly* will help scientists better understand these features on Titan.

The company SpaceX hopes to send people on missions to Mars someday. It is making new spacecraft to do this. One of the spacecraft is called Starship. This is a huge ship. The company says it could carry about 100 people. Someday it could land on Mars. People might live on Mars, instead of just visiting. This could be the most amazing space mission yet.

Scientists imagine a
future where people
might live on Mars.

MISSION CONTROL

Whenever a spacecraft leaves Earth, people at Mission Control are watching over it. These people are called flight controllers. They make sure every part of the mission is working as it should. For missions with astronauts, the flight controllers help the astronauts stay safe. They make sure the spacecraft is neither too hot nor too cold. They check that the astronauts have air to breathe. They help astronauts plan all the work they must do in space.

Flight controllers work on missions without people, too. They help steer probes and rovers. They make sure the spacecraft are working correctly. If something goes wrong, they have to figure out how to fix it. The flight controllers help make sure every mission goes according to plan.

▲
Mission Control is a room with many screens and computers to monitor missions.

GLOSSARY

astronauts (AS-troh-nots) Astronauts are people who go on missions in space. Some astronauts have gone to the moon.

drones (DROHNZ) Drones are small flying machines that people control remotely. A spacecraft called *Dragonfly* looks similar to the drones people fly on Earth.

orbit (OR-bit) An orbit is the round path that an object takes as it goes around a planet. Many space missions launch into orbit around Earth.

probes (PROHBZ) Probes are spacecraft without people inside. Probes such as *Cassini* are controlled by people back on Earth.

rocket (ROK-it) A rocket is a machine that launches things into space. A rocket called a Saturn V launched the Apollo 11 mission.

rovers (ROH-verz) Rovers are space probes with wheels that land on planets or moons and then drive around. The *Spirit* and *Opportunity* rovers were sent to Mars to explore the planet.

spacecraft (SPAYSS-kraft) A spacecraft is a machine that is made to fly in space. Some spacecraft carry people inside, and others are controlled from the ground.

TO LEARN MORE

IN THE LIBRARY

Carney, Elizabeth. *Mars: The Red Planet.*
Washington, DC: National Geographic Kids, 2016.

Hutchison, Patricia. *The First Moon Landing.*
Mankato, MN: The Child's World, 2016.

Morey, Allan. *Lunar Probes.* Minneapolis, MN:
Bellwether Media, 2018.

ON THE WEB

Visit our website for links about space missions:

childsworld.com/links

*Note to Parents, Teachers, and Librarians: We routinely verify
our Web links to make sure they are safe and active sites.
So encourage your readers to check them out!*

INDEX